Family Homes

Katie Peters

GRL Consultant Diane Craig,
Certified Literacy Specialist

Pull Ahead Readers

Lerner Publications ◆ Minneapolis

Note from a GRL Consultant
This Pull Ahead leveled book has been carefully designed for beginning readers. A team of guided reading literacy experts has reviewed and leveled the book to ensure readers pull ahead and experience success.

Lerner Publications
An imprint of Lerner Publishing Group, Inc.
241 First Avenue North
Minneapolis, MN 55401 USA

For reading levels and more information, look up this title at www.lernerbooks.com.

Main body text set in Memphis Pro 24/39
Typeface provided by Linotype.

Photo Acknowledgments
The images in this book are used with the permission of: © Ursula Page/Adobe Stock, p. 3; © Mostovyi Sergii Igorevich/Shutterstock, pp. 4–5; © Videoopps/Shutterstock, pp. 6–7; © AppleEyesStudio/Shutterstock, pp. 8–9, 16 (left); © Asada Nami/Shutterstock, pp. 10–11, 16 (middle); © Monkey Business Images/Shutterstock, pp. 12–13, 16 (right); © BGStock72/Shutterstock, pp. 14–15.

Front cover: © Monkey Business Images/Shutterstock

Library of Congress Cataloging-in-Publication Data

Names: Peters, Katie author
Title: Family homes / written by Katie Peters.
Description: Minneapolis : Lerner Publications, [2026] | Series: Let's look at families | Includes index. | Audience: Ages 4–7 | Audience: Grades K–1 | Summary: "From the desert to the mountains, home can look different for everyone. Leveled text helps readers explore how families live around the world. Pairs with the fiction story, Going to School Around the World"—Provided by publisher.
Identifiers: LCCN 2025011160 (print) | LCCN 2025011161 (ebook) | ISBN 9798765689851 library binding | ISBN 9798348028572 paperback | ISBN 9798765695067 epub
Subjects: LCSH: Families—Juvenile literature | Households—Juvenile literature
Classification: LCC HQ744 .P394 2026 (print) | LCC HQ744 (ebook) | DDC 306.85—dc23/eng/20250512

LC record available at https://lccn.loc.gov/2025011160
LC ebook record available at https://lccn.loc.gov/2025011161

Manufactured in the United States of America
1 – CG – 12/15/25

Table of Contents

Family Homes

We live in the mountains.

We live in the desert.

We live in the forest.

We live on a farm.

We live in a city.

Families live together everywhere.

Did You See It?

basket

chickens

stroller

Index